OXFORD
UNIVERSITY PRESS

Working in Films

Jessie Toms

Contents

Introduction

Have you ever stayed in the cinema after a film has ended? The list of names that comes after the film has ended is called the credits. All of the people listed in the credits have helped make the film. This book will show you what some of these people do. Or, as they say in the film industry, "Let's go behind the **scenes**."

Producer

The producer is in charge of all the business involved in making the film. A big film costs an enormous amount of money to produce. The producer has to make sure that it does not cost too much, and that the film is finished on time. The producer also chooses a director to make the film.

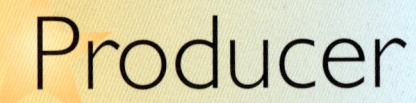

A film projector

Director

The director has to decide where the film will be made. This is called the location. It could be in any country in the world.

The director hires the actors, and everyone else needed to work on the film. This team is called the film crew. It includes everyone from the lighting person to the caterers who make the tea and sandwiches.

The director reads the whole film **script**. This shows all the words that the actors have to say. It also describes the actors' movements, and how they should look in each part of the film.

The director discusses the script with the producer.

★ The Film Shoot

Filming with a camera is called 'shooting' a film. The director shouts "Action" to start the filming. The cameras start running and the actors perform. The director will shout "Cut" to stop everybody if something does not look or sound right. One action may have to be shot again and again, until the director is satisfied with it and calls out "That's a wrap."

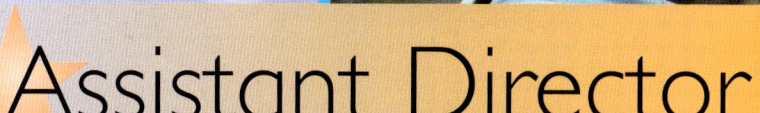

★Assistant Director

The assistant director helps the chief director by working out a plan for making the film. Every film is divided up into lots of small parts called **scenes**. They are all filmed separately and joined up later. Different actors will be needed at different times. The plan may be very complicated.

The assistant director also has to organize all the **film sets**. The sets are the separate stages where each **scene** is shot. Everything must be ready on the set before the shooting begins. All the things on the set are called the 'properties', or '**props**'.

A clapperboard snaps shut to show a new scene has started.

7

A model of a film set

Set Designer

The set designer uses a computer to draw plans of how the sets should look for each **scene**. He or she may also make small models of the sets.

Construction workers build the sets in the **studio**, following the designer´s plans. Building a **film set** can be very difficult, because everything must look real, even if it is only made from wood or plastic.

Set designers working on a set model

The casting director watches tapes of the actors' auditions.

⭐ Casting Director

The casting director makes a list of the best actors for the different roles in the film. The actors are invited to an **audition** where they act out a small part of the film. The casting director then decides which actors will be best to play the **characters** in the film. This is called casting.

It is the casting director's job to deal with the actor's **agent**. Together, they work out how much money the actor will be paid. They also agree what the actor can have during the filming.

Some actors ask for strange things. One actress once asked for a hairdresser for her dog. Another asked for a star to be put on his dressing room door. Famous actors almost always get what they want.

Actors waiting for filming to start

Actors

An actor's job is to pretend. They have to pretend they are the **character** in the film. Actors often have to learn a lot of lines for their **scenes** by heart. They sometimes have to learn to speak differently, too. If the actor is good you will believe that he or she really is the person in the story.

Sometimes extra people are needed to make a big crowd. They are called **extras**. They wear proper costumes but they do not have to learn lines.

Stunts are planned carefully before being performed.

Stunt People

Stunts are dangerous tricks. They make films exciting. A 'stunt double' often does a stunt in place of the real actor if the stunt is very dangerous. The stunt double is made up to look exactly like the actor. The audience will not even realize that a 'double' has been used in place of the actor.

Sometimes stunt people have to jump off ten-storey buildings, drive a car over a cliff or even get blown up.

Stunt people have to be well trained because doing stunts is very dangerous. They have to wear padding and safety harnesses so they do not get injured.

Stunt work is extremely dangerous.

Camera Operators

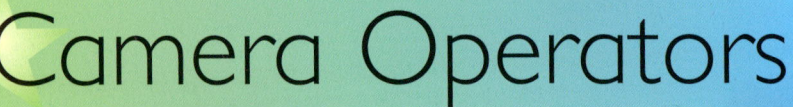

There are many camera operators on a **film set**. Their job is to photograph the action on moving film. They look through the camera lens and move the camera to follow the action. They will **shoot** each **scene** from different angles and in many ways.

It is important that camera operators know how each scene should look before shooting starts. The camera operators discuss the storyline and the scenes with the director and producer.

A camera operator waits for instructions from the director.

During a scene the camera operator follows the director's instructions. The director may ask for a 'close-up'. This is where the camera focuses on the face of an actor. Or the director may want a 'wide shot'. This is when the camera films the action from a distance showing the whole set.

A camera operator 'zooms in' for a close-up shot.

Costume Designer

The people that make or find the clothing worn by actors are called costume designers. The costumes are a very important part of a film because they help tell the story.

Costumes must fit with the film's story.

Each costume must be made to suit the **character** the actor is playing. They must also fit in with the storyline.

The costume designer has to think about each character´s part, and what year the story takes place in. The costumes would have to be old-fashioned for a film about the past, or they might have to look as if they come from the future. They could be costumes for a war film, or for make-believe characters.

19

Make-up Artist

How does that monster look so scary? How can that bruise look so real? Make-up artists can create amazing things with make-up. They can make actors look beautiful or scary.

Layer by layer the make-up artist builds up shapes with make-up. Sometimes the actors have to sit for hours having their make-up put on.

A make-up artist applies the finishing touches.

Actress Molly Ringwald before make-up is put on

Molly Ringwald wearing make-up for the part of 'Nicki the Twister' in the film *Spacehunter*

Next time you go to the cinema remember it is not just the actors who have made the film. Stay for a few minutes longer and have a look at the credits. They list some of the other behind-the-**scenes** jobs that go into making a film.

Glossary

agent - Someone who looks after an actor's or an author's business.

audition - A test to see if an actor is right for the part.

character - The person an actor must pretend to be.

extra - Someone who plays a background part in a film.

film set - The place where filming takes place.

props - Different items that may appear on stage or set, or that may be used by the actors.

scene - A part of a film.

script - The written text of a film.

shoot - To film a scene.

studio - The building where a film is made. It includes the sound stage and dressing rooms.

★ Index